ISBN 978-1-54394-036-7

1

These words are my raw, uncut autobiography

Stamped in stone with some photography

krussophotography

You are as beautiful as a rose

Even with thorns, your elegance shows

To you

This may be just a book

Another page with ink

But it is everything I've chosen to keep

A collection of emotions

My wandering mind

As each astrological sign changes with time

So did each thought I believed to be mine

To the one who cheated
Honesty was just a word to you
I am sorry I was not enough and you needed two

To the one who bruised
Make up could only cover so much
Tattoos now cover the scars

To the one who left without a word
Forever an open wound
Left staring at the moon

To the one who passed too soon
Your love has a place in my soul
Deep down to keep as my own

You made me cold

All emotions iced over

Forever waiting for the warmth of the sun

My heart is so heavy

With hurt

It drags behind

I crumbled

While you stood on two feet

I fell through the floor

While you stood above me

Nothing bad was happening

But nothing great was either

Neither of us wanted to let go

We knew once we did we would never hold each
other again

Maybe I waited too long to say how I felt

And by then it was too late for me

I waited and hoped you would have noticed

But you never did

People say that getting broken up with is the worst feeling, but nobody talks about how you would feel when you are the one ending a relationship. Granted, some people feel relief, or have already moved on. But what about the person who ended it all, and all it did was tear them to pieces just as much as the other person. When the relationship was not what was best for you, but all you wanted was for that person to be the one.

This is for that person.

The one who gave it everything they had, but it still did not work. And you know you still love them, but you somehow chose to let go of that great person standing in front of you

to stand

alone.

We screwed us up so bad

That I could not keep the one person I wanted to
stay

I expected more

Maybe more than you could offer

And for that I am sorry

You are not giving up

If you stayed you would be giving up on yourself

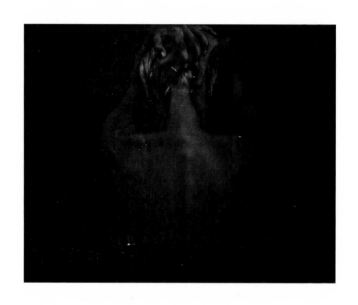

I thought my secrets were still mine

Even though I shared them with you

But now they are no longer my own

Even though they were never yours to loan

I told you all of my goals
And all of my dreams

I told you all of my fears
With streaming tears

It was all the little things that tore us apart

They continuously broke us down one at a time

Until all that was left were remains of what used to
be whole

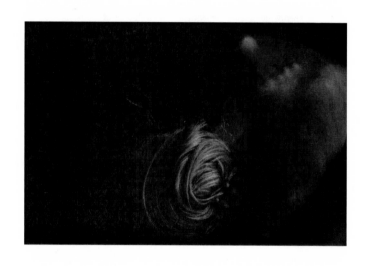

And you slowly release your breath

As your chest continues to cave in

Like a black hole in the middle of the galaxy

It grows deeper as air does not stop releasing from
your body

The darkness takes hold of your lungs capacity to
refill

Heaviness lies beneath the surface of your skin

Slowly adding pressure to your chest cavity

Suffocating your heart

My blood became a wildfire

Burning as it moved through my body

My mind became a tsunami

The water crashing and swallowing up all of our
memories

My heart became an avalanche

About to ice over

To you it was natural

But for me it was a disaster

-Natural Disaster

I thought that if you saw me again
You would change your mind

That if you saw my smile
There would be a next time

That if you felt the grip of my hug
You would never let it go

That if you heard my voice tremble
You would stay every day

That if you saw my tears
You would wipe them away

I thought that if you saw me in pain
You would try to take it all away

I thought that if you saw me again
You would want to stay

I sometimes wonder if you remember I am here
That all I wanted was for you to be near
I know you don't want me- you made that clear
But maybe one day you'll miss me,
my dear

My spine can no longer hold my body

My heart is too heavy

Even for this young body

My dreams are wearing thin

I might grab a bottle of gin

I know it is not the best option

But I choose my own sins

I came in this life

But knew I was never meant to live

When the time comes

Call my next of kin

My body became full of stress

It forced my mind to be a mess

Bottled to the top with emotion

I could no longer go to you as my magic potion

Where lightness fades
And darkness is manmade
Where every heart has been betrayed
Welcome to the devil's parade

Where you come to make a trade
And beg Hades to take their sun away
Where you ask him to start a crusade
Welcome to the devil's parade

Where you realize you are not afraid
And you go past your heart's blockade
Where you go after your love threw you a
homemade grenade
Welcome to the devil's parade

I had to do it on my own

Could no longer talk to you on the phone

Eventually the emotions came pouring out

Along with all of my self-doubt

After you

My home

Became my own

Skin and bones

I hope you watch the planes take off

And let your insecurities fly with them

I hope you take time to heal what was broken

So those sharp edges don't slice you open

I hope you find happiness in yourself

So you can give it to someone else

Laughing and talking all night

To things ending in a fight

We were once so close, our lives collided

Now we are strangers, calling others to confide in

Knowing our relationship will never be the same

Was a headache I forcefully overcame

The time came to undress someone new

I thought I was ready, but all I thought of was you

I went to trace my fingers over all of your tattoos

But it was on a body that did not belong to me

Or to you

You have strength built in

Release the heartache

Let the Life the Earth gave you begin

When the pieces are broken

All you want to do is put them back together

But sometimes the pieces are no longer pieces

They become ashes

Too small
to fit back together

So let them go

Put them back into the world

Give yourself peace

Too much has happened
To dare look back

But I hope you stare
Even if I can't

Let the past help you
With what you lack

Even if it puts me
In your past

Let go of what hurts

What is causing you pain

Even if you think it will destroy you

It tears your heart apart to stay

I will always wish you well

Every inch

Every cell

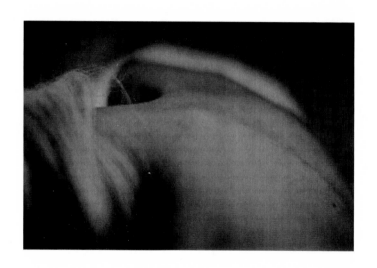

Everyone deserves the chance to move on
Especially us

But everyone else is moving around me
And I am stuck

You can drown out there

No matter how well you can swim
The current can take hold without a care
And your world will go dim
Even though it seems unfair

Do your best to stay afloat
Because surviving is rare
Do not rely on a boat
It may take more than just a prayer

But your courage will come out of nowhere

I will start over on the count of three

I have survived the darkness
I deserve to be free

Nobody saw my pain
I wouldn't let anyone see

That my heart crumbled
& became a pile of debris

I didn't believe in faith
But I begged on my knees
So nobody would have to write a eulogy for me

I have earned the right to keep going
I will not flee

I will create a new home within these bones
No need for a key
I am worthy of a life that is lovely and carefree

One
Two
Three

At your weakest point

Do not forget to be brave

Your soul is like a river

Flowing through a cave

And soon

You will be saved

I have rattled my own fears
To do the uncomfortable

I have pushed my body
To create new limits

I have torn people apart
To build new bridges

I have broken my own heart
To assemble a new soul

This is your race

Start a new pace

Bolt off the starting block

Throw out the lock

Jump over the first hurdle

Make it eternal

One done, don't stop

Whatever you do, stay on top

Sprint to the end

Make your heart mend

I can't tell you when you will feel like you are not
drowning anymore

Or when the waves will stop crashing into your
heart

The undertow will constantly pull you under,
flooding your mind

The water will fill you and smother your lungs

But keep looking up to the sun, you will reach the
surface

The water will disperse, and you will breathe deep
again

The tide will flow to land's edge, and your mind will
be free

The swells of the ocean will carry the pieces of your
heart back from the sea

Light up the sky

You already know how to fly

It may take time

But you will survive

Falling apart is not a crime

Eventually you will pick yourself up from the dive

Life is not always lemons

Sometimes it is limes

But do not forget you are human

You do not have nine lives

The person meant for you could be anywhere

They could be ten miles

Or across the Nile

I am the cold that comes with the snow

But even the arctic melts slowly

I am not a warm hearted person

But certain people spark **their own (a)** fire inside of me

Oh baby

This is my favorite song

So please don't come and do me wrong

You are like an old book in a thrift store

You have met a lot of people

And even called some of them your home

Your pages are not new

Maybe even a tear or two

But each wrinkle a chapter of a story told

About a soul learning to unfold

Maybe one day you will find out this is about you

And maybe, finally, you will feel my emotions too